PRESENTED TO

By

DATE

LEADERSHIP
PRINCIPLES

for

GRADUATES

CREATE SUCCESS IN LIFE
ONE DAY AT A TIME

JOHN C. MAXWELL

THOMAS NELSON
Since 1798

NASHVILLE   DALLAS   MEXICO CITY   RIO DE JANEIRO

Published in Nashville, Tennessee, by Thomas Nelson. Thomas Nelson is a registered trademark of Thomas Nelson, Inc.

Portions of *Leadership Principles for Graduates* were originally published as John C. Maxwell's *Success: One Day at a Time* (Nashville: Thomas Nelson, Inc., 2003).

Designed by The DesignWorks Group, Sisters, Oregon

ISBN 978-1-4041-0424-2

Published in association with Yates & Yates, www.yates2.com.

Printed and bound in Mexico
10 11 12 13 WC 9 8 7 6 5 4 3

You will never change your life
until you change something you
do daily.
    The secret of your success is
found in your daily routine.
                    —JOHN C. MAXWELL

PREFACE

Who *doesn't* desire success? It may seem peculiar to ask that question. Yet most of the people you know will never achieve success. They'll dream about it. They'll talk about it. But most of them won't possess it. And that's a shame. Why is that? Because most people don't understand success. It isn't the lottery. You don't stop at a convenience store on the way home, buy a ticket, and then wait for success to strike. Nor is it a place you find when you reach some magical time of life. Success is not a destination thing—it's a daily thing. The only way to achieve real success is to do it *one day at a time.*

THE TRUTH ABOUT SUCCESS

To be successful, you don't need to be lucky or rich. But you do need to know this:

- *You are what you do daily.*
- *You first form your habits; then your habits form you.*
- *It is just as easy to form habits of success as it is to form habits of failure.*

Every day you live, you are in the process of becoming. Whether you are becoming better or worse depends on what you give yourself to. Please allow me to give you some advice on how to make yourself successful.

SEVEN STEPS TO SUCCESS

1. COMMIT TO GROWING DAILY. One of the greatest mistakes people make is that they have the wrong focus. Success doesn't come from acquiring, achieving, or advancing. It comes only as the result of growing. If you make it your goal to grow a little every day, it won't be long before you begin to see positive results in your life. As the poet Robert Browning said, "Why stay on earth except to grow?"

2. VALUE THE PROCESS MORE THAN EVENTS. Specific life events are good for making decisions, but it's the process of change and growth that has lasting value. If you want to go to the next level, strive for continual improvement.

3. DON'T WAIT FOR INSPIRATION. Basketball great Jerry West said, "You can't get much done in life if you only work on the days when you feel good." The people who go far do so because they motivate themselves and give life their best, regardless of how they feel. To be successful, persevere.

4. BE WILLING TO SACRIFICE PLEASURE FOR OPPORTUNITY. One of the greatest lessons my father taught me was the principle of *pay now; play later.* For everything in life,

you pay a price. You choose whether you will pay it on the front end or the back end. If you pay first, then you will enjoy greater rewards in the end—and those rewards taste sweeter.

5. DREAM BIG. It doesn't pay to dream small. Robert J. Kriegel and Louis Patler, authors of *If It Ain't Broke, Break It*, assert, "We don't have a clue as to what people's limits are. All the tests, stopwatches, and finish lines in the world can't measure human potential. When someone is pursuing their dream, they'll go far beyond what seems to be their limitations. The potential that exists within us is limitless and largely untapped. When you think of limits, you create them."

6. PLAN YOUR PRIORITIES. One thing that all successful people have in common is that they have mastered the ability to manage their time. First and foremost, they have organized themselves. Henry Kaiser, founder of Kaiser Aluminum and Kaiser Permanente Health Care, says, "Every minute spent in planning will save you two in execution." You never regain lost time, so make the most of every moment.

7. GIVE UP TO GO UP. Nothing of value comes without sacrifice. Life is filled with critical moments when you

will have the opportunity to trade one thing you value for another. Keep your eyes open for such moments— and always be sure to trade up, not down.

If you dedicate yourself to these seven steps, then you will keep improving—and you will be successful. Your growth may not be obvious to others all at once, but you will see your progress almost immediately. And though recognition from others may come slowly, don't lose heart. Keep working at it. You will succeed in the end.

As you progress on this daily journey, use this book to jump-start your attitude and your insights. Read through the whole thing in a sitting or two. Then put it on your nightstand, in your car, or in your computer bag, satchel, or briefcase. When you have a moment, flip through its pages to remind you of what it means to achieve success.

It's going to be an incredible journey! Sometimes you will experience excitement; other times, only discipline will carry you through. But always remember: Success is waiting for you to make the first move. Let's get started.

JOHN C. MAXWELL
Spring 2007

Leadership is a choice you make,
not a place you sit.

—John C. Maxwell

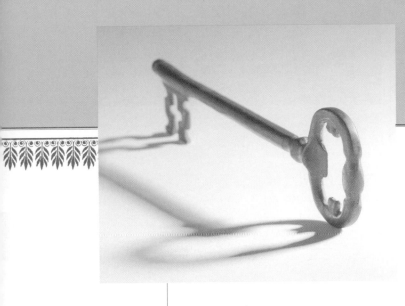

THE KEY TO SUCCESS

Many people who came before you searched for success and never found it. They thought of it as the Holy Grail or the Fountain of Youth—something to be captured at the end of a long quest. Some believed it was a relationship to be won. Others supposed it was a position to be earned or an object to be possessed.

But success is none of those things. It's not a destination to be reached. It is a process—a journey to be taken. And you do it one day at a time.

It takes most people some time to discover what they were created for. If you are willing, you can explore the world and learn more about your purpose every day. You can engage in activities that help you grow a little more in mind, body, or spirit. And you can perform some act—large or small—that helps others.

Success is knowing your purpose in life, sowing seeds that benefit others, and growing to your maximum potential.

The door to your potential is waiting for you. The key is to be on the journey. Keep at it day in and day out. If you are, you're a success today. And you'll be a success tomorrow.

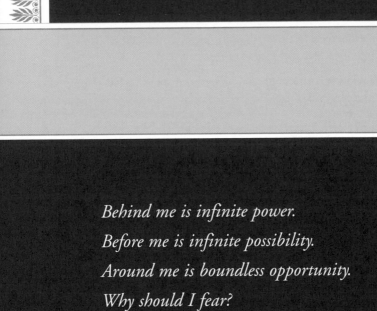

Behind me is infinite power.
Before me is infinite possibility.
Around me is boundless opportunity.
Why should I fear?

—STELLA STUART

DREAM EVERY DAY

Nurture Your 'Children'

D o you take care of your "children"? You may never have thought of your dreams as children, but that's what they are. They are your offspring—the joy of your today and the hope of your future. Protect them. Feed them. Nurture them. Encourage them to grow. Care for them. For someday, they may take care of you.

Cherish your visions
and your dreams as they are the
children of your soul;
the blueprints of your ultimate
achievements.
          —NAPOLEON HILL

Needed: People!

You cannot do it on your own. You will need the help of others—and you will need to give help to others—if you want to be successful. And that will require you to connect with others. To do that, follow these suggestions:

- *Focus on people.*
- *Be likable.*
- *Show others that you care.*
- *Remember everyone's name.*
- *Walk slowly through the crowd.*
- *Be generous.*

Seven Secrets of Success

1. There is no secret of success.

2. Success is for everyone.

3. Your life becomes better only when you become better.

4. There is no success without sacrifice.

5. Success is achieved in inches, not miles.

6. The greatest enemy of tomorrow's success is today's success.

7. No advice on success works unless you do.

OPPORTUNITIES ARE EVERYWHERE

A young man from the city graduated from college with a degree in journalism and got a job at a small-town newspaper. One of his first assignments was to interview an old farmer who lived twenty miles outside of town. As he sat with the grizzled man on his front porch, the young journalist looked at his notepad and started asking his questions. One of the first he asked was, "Sir, what time do you go to work in the morning?"

The old farmer chuckled and replied, "Son, I don't go to work. I'm surrounded by it."

We can learn a lesson from the old farmer. Opportunities are a lot like his work. They are everywhere. But the problem is that we often don't have the eyes to see them.

As you approach each day, look around. Be aware. If you don't see opportunities, remember that it's not because they aren't there. You're always surrounded by them. You simply need to open your eyes and see them. Then act on them.

Wanted!

More to *improve* and fewer to *disapprove*.

More *doers* and fewer *talkers*.

More to say *it can be done*
and fewer to say *it's impossible*.

More to *inspire* others
and fewer to *throw cold water* on them.

More to *get into the thick of things*
and fewer to *sit on the sidelines*.

More to point out *what's right*
and fewer to show *what's wrong*.

More to *light a candle*
and fewer to *curse the darkness*.

—Author Unknown

You will be as small as your
controlling desire, as great as your
dominant aspiration.

—James Allen

FIND YOUR VISION

O ne of the great dreamers of the twentieth century was Walt Disney. Any person who could create the first sound cartoon, first all-color cartoon, and first animated feature-length motion picture is definitely someone with vision. But Disney's greatest masterpieces of vision were Disneyland and Walt Disney World. And the spark for that vision came from an unexpected place.

Back when Walt's two daughters were young, he used to take them to an amusement park in the Los Angeles area on Saturday mornings. His girls loved it, and he did too. Amusement parks are a kid's paradise, with wonderful atmosphere: the smell of popcorn and cotton candy, the gaudy colors of signs advertising rides, and the sound of kids screaming as the roller coaster plummets over a hill.

Walt was especially captivated by the carousel. As he approached it, he saw a blur of bright images racing around to the tune of energetic calliope music. But when he got closer and the carousel stopped, he could see that his eye had been fooled. He observed shabby horses with cracked and chipped paint. And he noticed that only the horses on the outside row moved up and down. The others stood lifeless, bolted to the floor.

The cartoonist's disappointment inspired him with a grand vision. In his mind's eye he could see an amusement park where the illusion didn't evaporate, where children and adults could enjoy a carnival atmosphere without the seedy side that accompanies some circuses or traveling carnivals. His dream became Disneyland.

For Disney, vision was never a problem. Because of his creativity and desire for excellence, he always saw what could be. If you lack vision, look inside yourself. Draw on your natural gifts and desires. Look to your calling if you have one. And if you still don't sense a vision of your own, then consider hooking up with a leader whose vision resonates with you.

FROM *The 21 Indispensable Qualities of a Leader*

ONE STEP FURTHER

Do more than exist: *live.*

Do more than touch: *feel.*

Do more than look: *observe.*

Do more than read: *absorb.*

Do more than hear: *listen.*

Do more than listen: *understand.*

Do more than think: *reflect.*

Do more than just talk: *say something.*

—AUTHOR UNKNOWN

People who have given up
are ruled by their darkest mistakes, worst failures,
and deepest regrets. If you want to be successful,
then be governed by your finest thoughts,
your highest enthusiasm, your greatest optimism,
and your most triumphant experiences.

—JOHN C. MAXWELL

MRS. FIELD'S RECIPE FOR SUCCESS

Love what you're doing.
Believe in your product.
Select good people.
—DEBBI FIELDS

LEADERSHIP PRINCIPLES FOR GRADUATES

It's Easier

It's easier to settle for average
*   than strive for achievement.*

It's easier to be saturated with complacency
*   than stirred with compassion.*

It's easier to be skeptical
*   than successful.*

It's easier to question
*   than conquer.*

It's easier to rationalize your disappointments
*   than realize your dreams.*

It's easier to belch the baloney
*   than bring home the bacon.*

—Author Unknown

THE DOOR TO OPPORTUNITY

OPPORTUNITIES AND MOTIVATION ARE CONNECTED.
Motivated people see opportunities, and opportunities are
often what motivate people.

GREAT ATTITUDES PRECEDE GREAT OPPORTUNITIES.
Who you are determines what you see.

TODAY IS THE BEST DAY FOR AN OPPORTUNITY.
Opportunity always takes "now" for an answer.

OPPORTUNITIES ARE THE RESULT OF PLUCK, NOT LUCK.
The people who succeed seek out opportunities, and if
they can't find them, they create them.

OPPORTUNITIES DON'T PRESENT THEMSELVES IN IDEAL
CIRCUMSTANCES. If you wait for all the lights to turn
green, you will never leave your driveway.

OPPORTUNITY WITHOUT COMMITMENT WILL BE LOST.
Abandoned opportunities are never lost—they are simply
pursued by the competition.

OPPORTUNITY IS BIRTHED OUT OF PROBLEMS. If you're
looking for a BIG opportunity, find a BIG problem.

OPPORTUNITIES EITHER MULTIPLY OR DISAPPEAR. The more
opportunities you pursue, the more you find behind them.

OPPORTUNITIES MUST BE NOURISHED IF THEY ARE TO
SURVIVE. As Peter Drucker, the father of modern
management, says, "Feed an opportunity; starve a problem."

To do a common thing
uncommonly well
brings success.
—HENRY JOHN HEINZ

To laugh often and much;
to win the respect of intelligent people
and the affection of children,
to earn the appreciation of honest critics
and endure the betrayal of false friends;
to appreciate beauty, to find the best in others,
to leave the world a bit better
whether by a healthy child, a garden patch,
or a redeemed social condition;
to know even one life has breathed easier
because you lived.
This is to have succeeded.

—RALPH WALDO EMERSON

Life is either
a daring adventure
or nothing at all.
Security is mostly
a superstition.
It does not exist in nature.

—HELEN KELLER

Cautious, careful people,
always casting about to preserve their
reputation and social standing,
never can bring about a reform.
Those who are really in earnest
must be willing to be anything or nothing
in the world's estimation,
and publicly and privately,
in season and out,
avow their sympathy with despised
and persecuted ideas and their advocates,
and bear the consequences.

—SUSAN B. ANTHONY

I Dare You to Try

Sometimes we don't know what we want until someone tells us we can't have it. That's what happened with Oliver Wendell Holmes, Jr. He was wounded three times during the Civil War, and while home on medical leave he decided to go to law school. His father, a renowned physician who dominated his family, scorned the young man's decision. "What's the use of that? A lawyer can't become a great man." Many years later, while still serving on the U.S. Supreme Court at the age of ninety, Holmes recalled his father's words and how they spurred him to pursue his dream and prove his worth as a lawyer.

We cannot achieve our wildest dreams
by remaining who we are.

—John C. Maxwell

Keep your goals out of reach but not out of sight.

—Author Unknown

THE DA VINCI DREAMS

L eonardo da Dinci was a dreamer. While apprenticed to a prominent artist in Florence, Italy, he learned among the best and brightest of the time and had access to the most powerful patrons of the emerging Renaissance.

But Leonardo's circumstances aren't what made him great. His dreams did. From his youth he'd kept notebooks of inventions that he'd dreamed up, natural forms that he'd observed, and even short stories—all things that fired his imagination and his thirst to learn more about the world. The few notebooks that have survived since his death in 1519 show us the genius of a visionary far ahead of his time. The technologies and financial support needed to implement his ideas were still centuries away from being available. Gliders, scuba gear, parachutes, water pumps, bicycles, mechanical looms, cannons, portable bridges, helicopters, musical instruments, a calculator, even a robot—variations of these were among his ideas, and many have been crafted in modern times to prove that they worked perfectly.

The world wasn't ready for most of Leonardo's dreams. But he kept dreaming.

Your colleagues and friends won't always be ready for your ideas. But you must keep imagining. Write down what you envision, refine your ideas, and when the right moment comes, take action to bring your dreams to life.

THE GREATEST GENERAL

A man died and met Saint Peter at the gates of heaven. Recognizing the saint's knowledge and wisdom, he wanted to ask him a question.

"Saint Peter," he said, "I have been interested in military history for many years. Tell me, who was the greatest general of all times?"

Peter quickly responded, "Oh, that is a simple question. It's that man right over there."

The man looked where Peter was pointing and answered, "You must be mistaken. I knew that man on earth, and he was just a common laborer."

"That's right," Peter remarked, "but he would have been the greatest general of all time—if he had been a general."

—MARK TWAIN

ALL YOU CAN

Do all the good you can,
By all the means you can,
In all the ways you can,
In all the places you can,
At all the times you can,
To all the people you can,
As long as ever you can.

—JOHN WESLEY

It is your duty to find yourself.

—JOHN C. MAXWELL

Pursue Your Passion

Elizabeth Blackwell decided to pursue a career in medicine after a dying friend confessed that she might have sought treatment sooner if a woman doctor had been available. However, many obstacles lay in her way: she lacked money, she lacked the education necessary for admittance to medical school, and she was a single woman living in the mid-1800s. No woman had ever been accepted to medical school, and no doctor believed she could succeed.

Persistent in her dream, Elizabeth convinced a doctor to teach her privately and let her use his personal library to prepare for medical school. After dozens of rejections, a small medical school in Geneva, New York, agreed to let her join the class under one condition: the other students had to agree. Thinking it was a joke, the students unanimously agreed to admit her, and on November 6, 1847, Elizabeth took her place in the class. She endured not only the grueling work, but also the curiosity and outright scorn of onlookers. Hospitals refused to permit her hands-on training, so she worked among the poverty-stricken ill and insane of Philadelphia instead.

In 1849, Elizabeth graduated first in her class, having won the respect of teachers, classmates, and townfolk.

But more battles lay ahead. Newspapers throughout the United States and Europe mocked or vilified both Elizabeth and Geneva Medical College. When Elizabeth sought additional training in Paris and London, she had to face the same obstacles there that she had in America. When she established her practice back in New York, patients were slow in coming, so she responded by opening her own medical college that treated indigent women and children while training female doctors and nurses. This institution still exists as the New York University Downtown Hospital, where more than 1,500 people were treated after the September 11, 2001, attack on the World Trade Center.

Elizabeth pursued her passion, and she made a tremendous difference—in her own life, in the lives of other women who have followed her into the medical profession, and in the lives of the countless people who have benefited from women's medical expertise.

What's your dream? What are you doing about it? Be persistent in your passion!

Exercise for Success

Think of the pursuit of your dream as being like a major athletic event. Train for it. As you prepare and "exercise," you will get stronger—mentally, emotionally, and physically. To successfully achieve your dream, you need to keep improving. The best way to do that is to . . .

• keep your body fit.
• keep your heart flexible.
• keep your mind open.
• keep your comfort zone expanding.

Everybody can be great . . .
        because anybody can serve.
You don't have to have a college degree to serve.
You don't have to make your subject and verb agree
        to serve.
You only need a heart full of grace.
A soul generated by love.

—MARTIN LUTHER KING JR.

All the beautiful sentiments in the world
weigh less than a single lovely action.

—JAMES RUSSELL LOWELL

KEYS TO SUCCESS

Most men die from the neck up
at age twenty-five
because they stop dreaming.

—BEN FRANKLIN

Those closest to you
will stretch your vision
or choke your dreams.

—JOHN C. MAXWELL

You will invest your life in something,
Or you will throw it away on nothing.

—HADDON ROBINSON

Never give up then,
for that is just the place and time
that the tide will turn.
—Harriett Beecher Stowe

PERSEVERE EVERY DAY

Do Yourself a Favor

A poor, hungry young man sat moping on a bridge, watching a group of fishermen. Looking into a basket and seeing a bunch of fish nearby, the young man said, "Boy, if I had a mess of fish like that, I'd be in good shape. I'd sell them and buy some clothes and something to eat."

"I'll give you that many fish if you do a small favor for me," a fisherman replied.

"Sure."

"Tend this line for me awhile. I've got some errands to do up the street," said the older man.

The young man gladly accepted the offer. As he tended the man's pole, the fish were really biting, and he reeled in one fish after another. It wasn't long before he was smiling, enjoying the activity.

When the older man returned, he said, "I want to give you the fish I promised. Here, take all the fish you caught. But I also want to give you a piece of advice. The next time you're in need, don't waste time daydreaming and wishing for what could be. Get busy, cast the line yourself, and make something happen."

A Thorn in Your Side?

As you discover your purpose in life and pursue your dreams, you will inevitably spend more and more of your time doing what you enjoy and do best.

That's good. You can achieve your dreams only if you focus on your priorities.

But success requires something else: discipline. One of the best ways I know to improve discipline is to do something you don't enjoy doing—every day. If you learn to do what you must, you will be able to do what you want.

Do something you hate every day,
 just for the practice.
                    —John C. Maxwell

Success seems to be connected with action. Successful people keep moving. They make mistakes, but they don't quit.

—CONRAD HILTON

KEYS TO SUCCESS

Nothing in the world
can take the place of persistence.
Talent will not—
nothing is more common
than unsuccessful men with talent.
Genius will not—
unrewarded genius is almost a proverb.
Education will not—
the world is full of educated derelicts.
Persistence and determination alone
are omnipotent.

—PRESIDENT CALVIN COOLIDGE

You'll never plow a field
by turning it over in your mind.

—IRISH PROVERB

Long-Term Success

All U.S. schoolchildren know about the success of Abraham Lincoln. His phenomenal leadership of the United States guided the nation through the devastating Civil War. But few teachers talk about Lincoln's many failures as well as victories on the way to the presidency.

1831—His business went bankrupt.

1832—He was defeated in a legislative race.

1833—Another business failed.

1834—He was elected to the Illinois legislature.

1835—His fiancée died.

1836—He had a nervous breakdown.

1842—He married Mary Todd, whose family had a wider network of social and political connections.

1843—He was defeated in a Congressional race.

1847   He was elected to serve in the House of Representatives.

1848—He was defeated in another Congressional race.

1855—He was defeated in a Senatorial race.

1856—He was defeated in a vice presidential bid.

1860—He was elected the sixteenth president of the United States.

Three decades of dealing with both victory and defeat prepared Lincoln for the daily trials of leading the nation through terrible war. The resilient attitude he developed during his own difficulties enabled him to wisely, compassionately guide the United States through its darkest era.

Success is going from
failure to failure
without losing your enthusiasm.
— Abraham Lincoln

If you keep doing
what you've always done,
you'll always get
what you've always gotten.
— John C. Maxwell

There are no shortcuts
to any place worth going.
——Beverly Sills

Opportunity is missed by most people because it is
dressed in overalls and looks like work.
——Thomas Edison

Show me a man
who cannot bother
to do little things,
and I'll show you a man
who cannot be trusted
to do big things.
——Lawrence D. Bell

He who is afraid of doing too much always does too little.
——German Proverb

There is no defeat except in no longer trying. There is no defeat save within, no really insurmountable barrier, save our own inherent weakness of purpose.

—Elbert Hubbard

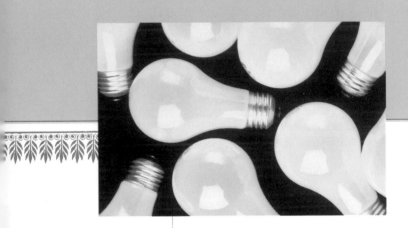

LONG ON IDEAS

ife magazine named him the number one man of the millennium. The number of things he invented is astounding—1,093. He held more patents than any other person in the world, having been granted at least one patent every year for sixty-five consecutive years. His name was Thomas Edison.

Most people credit Edison's ability to creative genius. He credited it to hard work. "Genius," he declared, "is ninety-nine percent perspiration and one percent inspiration." I believe his success was also the result of a third factor: his positive attitude.

Edison was an optimist who saw the best in everything. "If we did all the things we were capable of doing," he once said, "we would literally astound ourselves." When it took him ten thousand tries to find the right materials for the incandescent light bulb, he didn't see them as that many failures. With each attempt he gained information about what didn't work, bringing him closer to a solution. He never doubted that he would find a good one. His belief could be summarized by his statement: "Many of life's failures are people who did not realize how close they were to success when they gave up."

Probably the most notable display of Edison's positive attitude can be seen in the way he approached a tragedy that occurred when he was in his late sixties. The lab he had built in West Orange, New Jersey, was world famous. He called the fourteen-building complex his invention factory. Its main building was massive—greater than three football fields in size. From that base of operations, he and his staff conceived of inventions, developed prototypes, manufactured products, and shipped them to customers. It became a model for modern research and manufacturing.

Edison loved the place. . . . But on a December day in 1914, his beloved lab caught fire. As he stood outside and watched it burn, he is reported to have said, "Kids, go get your mother. She'll never see another fire like this one."

Most people would have been crushed. Not Edison. "I am sixty-seven," he said after the tragedy, "but not too old to make a fresh start. I've been through a lot of things like this." He rebuilt the lab, and he kept working for another seventeen years. "I am long on ideas, but short on time," he commented. "I expect to live to be only about a hundred." He died at age eighty-four.

If Edison hadn't been such a positive person, he never would have achieved such success as an inventor. If you look at the lives of people in any profession who achieve lasting success, you will find that they almost always possess a positive outlook on life.

FROM *The 21 Indispensable Qualities of a Leader*

KEYS TO SUCCESS

Failure is really a matter of conceit.
People don't work hard because,
in their conceit, they imagine they'll succeed
without ever making an effort.
Most people believe that they'll
wake up some day and find themselves rich.
Actually, they've got it half right,
because eventually they do wake up.

—THOMAS EDISON

The world stands aside
to let anyone pass who knows
where he is going.

   —DAVID STARR GORDON

I am willing to put myself through anything;
temporary pain or discomfort means nothing to me
as long as I can see that the experience
will take me to a new level.
I am interested in the unknown,
and the only path to the unknown
is through breaking barriers,
an often-painful process.

      —DIANA NYAD

KEYS TO SUCCESS

Success is not measured
by what a man accomplishes,
but by the opposition he has encountered,
and the courage with which he
has maintained the struggle
against overwhelming odds.

—CHARLES LINDBERGH

THE WAY TO THE TOP

My friend Zig Ziglar once told me that he visited the Washington Monument on a trip to Washington, D.C. As he arrived with some friends, he heard a guide announce, "Ladies and gentlemen, there is currently a two-hour wait to ride the elevator to the top of the monument." The guide then paused a moment, smiled, and added, "However, there is *no wait* should you desire to take the stairs."

Zig's story reveals something about success. In truth, there are no elevators to the top. If you want to make it there, you've got to take a long series of steps. How many steps you're willing to take—and how long you're willing to keep climbing—determines how high you will go.

I am a great believer in luck,
and I find that the harder I work,
the more I have of it.

—STEPHEN LEACOCK

GENIUS!

Sarasate, the greatest
Spanish violinist of the nineteenth century,
was once called a genius by a famous critic.
In reply to this, Sarasate declared,
"Genius! For thirty-seven years
I've practiced fourteen hours a day,
and now they call me a genius."

You can become the star of the hour
if you make the minutes count.
—AUTHOR UNKNOWN

Every worthwhile accomplishment
has a price tag attached to it.
The question is always whether you
are willing to pay the price to attain it—
in hard work, sacrifice, patience,
faith, and endurance.
—JOHN C. MAXWELL

A year from now
you may wish
you had started today.
—KAREN LAMB

PERSIST IN FILLING YOUR LIST

Every leader's potential is determined by the people closest to him or her. If those people are strong, then the leader can make a huge impact. If they are weak, the leader can accomplish very little.

As you consider your journey toward ever-greater leadership, you'll need good companions. Your inner circle will make you or break you. Several years ago I created a list of the kinds of people who help me, according to the ways that they add value to my life, and I suggest that you start forming a similar circle of companions. Some especially valuable people will fulfill multiple roles. The right list of inner-circle advisors isn't always easy to find, but keep looking. It'll be worth it!

Celebrator. When you accomplish your goals, take a moment to celebrate with the people who helped you win.

Creator. Creative people stretch your mind, challenge your direction, increase your vision, and multiply your gifts.

Defender. On the days when you're too weary to fight you own battles, having someone who will step into the ring for you is a real blessing.

Discerner. No matter how good you are, you will always miss some details when making decisions. Partner with people who will see what you don't.

Encourager. Even people with great attitudes sometimes become discouraged. Encouragement is like oxygen to the soul.

Giver. Your life should be focused on giving to others. But to keep giving, you also will need to have your "tank" filled. Connect with someone who loves you unconditionally.

Implementer. Marshall McLuhan observed: "After all has been said and done, more will have been said than done." Implementers are the people who get things done.

Intercessor. You need someone to pray for you. Without God's favor and blessing you can do nothing of value.

Listener. Everyone needs a friendly ear to confide in, vent to, and bounce ideas off.

Mentor. No matter how advanced you are in your leadership, others ahead of you can help you along the way.

Networker. It has been said that you are five people away from contacting anyone in the world. Find a good networker and you're only two away.

Protégé. If you have leadership ability, you've not been given it to hoard for yourself. Find the right person to pour your life into.

Resourcer. Every year I speak to 250,000 people and write at least one book. That requires lots of preparation. I'm grateful to the people willing to help me.

Sponsor. You can't pick your sponsor; he or she has to pick you. Pray for God to put people in your life who will believe in you and use their influence to help you.

Thinker. Some people are talented at solving problems. Everybody needs someone who can do that.

FROM *The 21 Most Powerful Minutes in a Leader's Day*

By perseverance
the snail reached the ark.
—CHARLES H. SPURGEON

Success is a little like wrestling a gorilla.
You don't quit when you're tired—
you quit when the gorilla is tired.
—ROBERT STRAUSS

It takes twenty years
to make an overnight success.
—EDDIE CANTOR

THEY CALLED IT LUCK

He worked by day
and toiled by night.
He gave up play
and much delight.
Dry books he read,
new things to learn.
And forged ahead,
success to earn.
He plodded on,
with faith and pluck.
And when he won,
they called it luck.

—AUTHOR UNKNOWN

Not *realizing* what you want
    is a problem of *knowledge*.
Not *pursuing* what you want
    is a problem of *motivation*.
Not *achieving* what you want
    is a problem of *persistence*.

—JOHN C. MAXWELL

WIN THE DAILY BATTLE

People who achieve daily success have learned
to conquer four common time-wasters.

LAZINESS:
Time put to no useful purpose,
not even relaxation.

PROCRASTINATION:
Putting off things that should be done now.

DISTRACTION:
Time frittered away on the
details of side issues,
to the detriment of the main
issue.

IMPATIENCE:
Lack of preparation,
thoroughness,
or perseverance, usually
resulting
in time-consuming mistakes.

Do It Today

Do the right thing;
Do it today;
Do it with no hope of return or promise of reward;
Do it with a smile and a cheerful attitude;
Do it day after day after day.
Do it, and someday,
There will come a day
That will be a payday
For all the yesterdays
You spent focused on the current day—
That will not only give value to today,
But will make each future day
Outshine each yesterday.
And what more could you ask of a day?

You can't build a reputation on what you are going to do.

—HENRY FORD

If you wish success in life,
make perseverance your bosom friend,
experience your wise counselor,
caution your elder brother and
hope your guardian genius.

—JOSEPH ADDISON

The happiness of a man in this life
does not consist in the absence but
in the mastery of his passions.

—ALFRED LORD TENNYSON

THE EIGHT "P" PLAN FOR ACHIEVEMENT

Plan Purposefully.

Prepare Properly.

Proceed Positively.

Pursue Persistently.

—AUTHOR UNKNOWN

Success is 99 percent failure.

—SOICHIRO HONDA

It's so simple that it's revolutionary. The fact is, this formula or principle is misunderstood enough, or overlooked enough, that it can truly be called magic by those who understand it. Ready? Here it is.

You beat 50 percent of the people in America by working hard.

You beat another 40 percent by being a person of honesty and integrity and standing for something.

The last 10 percent is a dogfight in the free enterprise system.

—ART WILLIAMS

A success is one who decided to succeed—
and *worked.*
A failure is one who decided to succeed—
and *wished.*
A decided failure is one who failed to decide—
and *waited.*

—WILLIAM A. WARD

Far better it is to dare mighty things,
to win glorious triumphs,
even though checkered with failure,
than to take rank with those poor spirits
who neither enjoy much nor suffer much
because they live in the gray twilight
that knows not victory nor defeat.

—THEODORE ROOSEVELT

How to Spell
S-U-C-C-E-S-S

Select your goal.

Unlock your personal potential.

Commit yourself to your plan.

Chart your course.

Expect problems.

Stand firm on your commitment.

Share the rewards with others.

Stop what you're doing
long enough to grow.
—JOHN C. MAXWELL

GROW EVERY DAY

Success is never final.

People who reach their potential
spend more time asking,
"what am I doing well?"
rather than
"what am I doing wrong?"

—JOHN C. MAXWELL

GROW TO YOUR POTENTIAL

It's been said that our potential is God's gift to us, and what we do with it is our gift to him. But our potential is probably our greatest untapped resource. Why? We can do anything, but we can't do everything. Many people never really dedicate themselves to their purpose in life. They become a jack of all trades, master of none—rather than a jack of few trades, focused on one.

Here are four principles to put you on the road to growing toward your potential:

1. CONCENTRATE ON ONE MAIN GOAL. Nobody ever reached their potential by scattering themselves in twenty directions. Reaching your potential requires focus.

2. CONCENTRATE ON CONTINUAL IMPROVEMENT. Commitment to continual improvement is the key to reaching our potential. Each day you can become a little bit better than you were yesterday.

3. FORGET THE PAST. Maybe you've made a lot of mistakes in your life, or you've had an especially difficult past. Work your way through it and move on.

4. FOCUS ON THE FUTURE. You can become better tomorrow than you are today. As the Spanish proverb says, "He who does not look ahead remains behind."

FROM *Your Road Map for Success*

Which Way Are You Driving?

People typically have two conflicting bents when it comes to their work:

The first is the drive *to have*. It pushes people to focus on what they can get out of their jobs—a higher salary, a bigger office, greater status, a better position.

The second is the desire *to be*. It prompts people to think about what they can give to their organizations—their very best to ensure that everyone succeeds.

Formula for Success

Instruction + Example x Experience = Success

KEYS TO SUCCESS

Without rest,
a man cannot work.
Without work,
the rest does not
give you any benefit.
—ABKHASIAN PROVERB

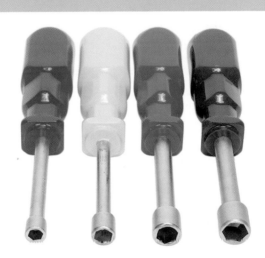

R-E-A-L Success

I believe that to succeed, a person needs only four things. You can remember them by thinking of the word REAL.

Relationships: The greatest skill needed for success is the ability to get along with other people. It impacts every aspect of a person's life. Your relationships make you or break you.

Equipping. One of the greatest lessons I've learned in life is that those closest to you determine the level of your success. If your dreams are great, you achieve them only with a team.

Attitude: People's attitudes determine how they approach life day-to-day. Your attitude, more than your aptitude, will determine your altitude.

Leadership: Everything rises and falls on leadership. If you desire to "lift the lid" on your personal effectiveness, the only way to do it is to increase your leadership skills.

If you dedicate yourself to growing in these four areas, then it doesn't matter what kind of work you do. You will become successful.

FROM *Failing Forward*

TEN TRADE-OFFS
WORTH MAKING

1. TRADE THE FIRST HALF FOR THE SECOND HALF. Much of the first half of life is spent paying the price for later success. The greater dues you pay now, the more they compound, and the greater potential for a successful second half.

2. TRADE AFFIRMATION FOR ACCOMPLISHMENT. Accolades fade quickly, but your accomplishments have the potential to make a positive impact on the lives of others.

3. TRADE FINANCIAL GAIN FOR FUTURE POTENTIAL. The temptation is almost always to go for the "big bucks." But seeking to have greater potential almost always leads to a higher return—including financially.

4. TRADE IMMEDIATE PLEASURE FOR PERSONAL GROWTH. An oak tree requires decades to grow, but a squash only takes weeks. Which do you want to be?

5. TRADE EXPLORATION FOR FOCUS. The younger you are, the more experimenting you should do. But once you've found what you were created to do, stick with it.

6. **TRADE QUANTITY OF LIFE FOR QUALITY OF LIFE.** Your life is not a dress rehearsal. Give it your best because you won't get another chance.

7. **TRADE SECURITY FOR SIGNIFICANCE.** The great men and women of history were great not because of what they owned or earned, but because they gave their lives to accomplish greatness.

8. **TRADE ACCEPTABLE FOR EXCELLENCE.** If something is worth doing, either give it your best or don't do it at all.

9. **TRADE ADDITION FOR MULTIPLICATION.** When you invest in others, you multiply your efforts—every person you assist becomes a fellow workmate.

10. **TRADE AMBITION FOR GRATITUDE.** Anyone who succeeds does so because of the help and grace of others. Be grateful for everything you have, and share it with others.

KEYS TO SUCCESS

You have reached the pinnacle of success
as soon as you become uninterested
in money, compliments, or publicity.

—O. A. BATTISTA

Life is not easy for any of us.
But what of that?
We must have perseverance
and, above all, confidence in ourselves.
We must believe
that we are gifted for something
and that this thing must be attained.

—MARIE CURIE

My doctors told me I would never walk again.
My mother told me I would.
I believed my mother.

—WILMA RUDOLPH
OLYMPIC GOLD MEDALIST

BECOME THE TEAM PLAYER EVERYONE WANTS

Few people leap directly to leading a team after they receive a diploma. Instead, graduates must prove themselves as excellent team players before they achieve opportunities to advance. All people can choose to become better teammates by embodying the qualities of a team player. Do that yourself, help your teammates do the same, and the whole team will excel. Team players strive to be . . .

1. ADAPTABLE. You must be willing to adapt to the team instead of expecting the team to adapt to you.

2. COLLABORATIVE. When *completing* each other is more important than *competing* with each other, your contributions aren't merely added to the team; they're multiplied.

3. COMMITTED. There are no halfhearted champions.

4. COMMUNICATIVE. A team is many voices with a single heart. If you're not communicating with other team members, the whole team suffers.

5. COMPETENT. Highly competent people are committed to excellence. They refuse the merely average, pay attention to detail, and perform with consistency.

6. DEPENDABLE. Are you a go-to player, or do your teammates work around you when crunch time comes?

7. DISCIPLINED. By disciplining your thinking, emotions, and actions, you're paying the price in the little things so that you can attain the bigger things.

8. **Enlarging.** Nothing is as valuable—or rewarding—as adding value to the lives of others.

9. **Enthusiastic.** Enthusiasm energizes the team, and that energy produces the power to accomplish even the most difficult tasks.

10. **Intentional.** Focus on the right things, moment to moment, day to day, and then follow through with them in a consistent, productive way.

11. **Mission Conscious.** See more than the details of the moment, remain conscious of the team's mission, and act to help achieve it.

12. **Prepared.** Courage has no greater ally than preparation, and fear has no greater enemy.

13. **Relational.** Relationships are the glue that holds a team together.

14. **Self-Improving.** Don't wait for circumstances or another person to improve you. You must take responsibility for that yourself.

15. **Selfless.** No team succeeds unless its players put others on the team ahead of themselves.

16. **Solution Oriented.** Do you see a solution in every challenge or a problem in every circumstance? There are only four choices in handling problems: flee them, fight them, forget them, or face them. Which do you do?

17. **Tenacious.** You haven't won the race until you've crossed the finish line.

FROM *The 17 Essential Qualities of a Team Player*

Success is a continuing thing.
It is growth and development.
It is achieving one thing and using
that as a stepping stone to achieve
something else.

—JOHN C. MAXWELL

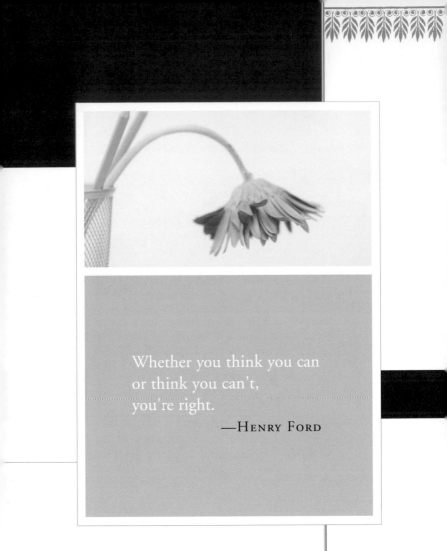

Whether you think you can
or think you can't,
you're right.

—HENRY FORD

Six Habits of Highly Defective People

1. THEY HAVE A LOSING ATTITUDE. People generally get whatever they expect out of life. Expect the worst, and that's what you'll get.

2. THEY QUIT GROWING. People are what they are, and they are where they are because of what has gone into their minds.

3. THEY HAVE NO GAME PLAN FOR LIFE. As William Feather, author of *The Business of Life*, says, "There are two kinds of failures: Those who thought and never did, and those who did and never thought."

4. THEY ARE UNWILLING TO CHANGE. Some people would rather cling to what they hate rather than embrace what might be better because they are afraid of getting something worse.

5. THEY FAIL IN RELATIONSHIPS WITH OTHERS. People who cannot get along with others will never get ahead in life.

6. THEY ARE NOT WILLING TO PAY THE PRICE FOR SUCCESS. The road to success is uphill all the way. Anyone who wants to accomplish much must sacrifice much.

BIRDS OF A FEATHER

For years, Monterey, California, was a pelican's paradise. The town was the site of many fish canneries. In fact, it was the home of Cannery Row, a street popularized by Nobel Prize-winning author John Steinbeck in his novel of that name.

Pelicans loved the town because fisherman cleaned their catch, discarding the offal, and the pelicans would feast on those scraps. In Monterey, any pelican could be well fed without having to work for a meal.

But as time went by, the fish along the California coast were depleted, and one by one, the canneries all shut down. That's when the pelicans got into trouble. You see, pelicans are naturally great fishers. They fly in groups over the waves of the sea, and when they find fish, they dive into the water and scoop up their catch. But these pelicans hadn't fished in years. They had grown fat and lazy. And now that their easy meals were gone, they were actually starving.

Environmentalists from the area wracked their brains to figure out a way to help the pelicans, and finally they came up with a solution. They imported pelicans from another area, ones that were used to foraging every day, and they mixed them in with the local birds. The newcomers immediately started fishing for their own food, and it wasn't long before the starving native birds joined them and started fishing for themselves again.

If you find yourself starving for success, one of the best ways to get things going in your life is to be around people who are achieving success. Spend time with them. Watch how they work. Learn how they think. You will inevitably become like the people you are around.

It's right to be content with what you have,
but not with what you are.

—AUTHOR UNKNOWN

The highest reward for your work
is not what you get for it,
but what you become by it.
—JOHN C. MAXWELL

Keys to Success

Where Do You Live?

Young people live in the future.
Old people live in the past.
Wise people live in the present.

TIME ON YOUR HANDS

L ook at your day. How do you spend it? What ruts have you gotten yourself into that you could easily break yourself out of? What poor habits are eating valuable minutes of your life every day?

What impact can a few minutes make? Take a look at this. What if you were able to save . . .

FIVE MINUTES by streamlining your morning routine (taking less time to dress, shave, put on makeup, drink coffee, read the paper, and so on)?

TEN MINUTES by eliminating the things you do each morning to stall starting your work or school day?

FIVE MINUTES by avoiding idle talkers or other distractions?

TEN MINUTES by taking a shorter lunch or break time? Those minutes don't seem like much. But if you did those things every day, five days a week, for fifty weeks, you would gain an additional 125 hours of time every year. (That's the equivalent of more than *three forty-hour weeks* to use for anything you want!) And if you're a television watcher, you can *double* the time you gain each year if you simply watch thirty fewer minutes of television every day.

Time is usually wasted
in the same way every day.
—PAUL MEYER

THE TOP TEN HIGH-VALUE USES OF YOUR TIME

1. Things that advance your overall life purpose.
2. Things you have always wanted to do.
3. Things that others say can't be done.
4. Things that help you grow to your maximum potential.
5. Things that develop other people's ability to achieve and lead.
6. Things that multiply—rather than merely add—value to yourself and others.
7. Things that harness your creativity.
8. Things you can delegate to others.
9. Things that promote teamwork and synergy.
10. Things that are *now or never* opportunities.

Success is not perfection;
success is slightly above average.

—Author Unknown

Life is like riding in a taxi.
Whether you are going anywhere or not,
the meter keeps ticking.

—John C. Maxwell

It's Not about Money

Wealth—and what it brings—is at best fleeting. For example, in 1923, a small group of the world's wealthiest men met at the Edgewater Beach Hotel in Chicago, Illinois. They were a "Who's Who" of wealth and power. Here's a list of who was there and what eventually happened to them:

CHARLES M. SCHWAB: president of the largest independent steel company—died broke.

ARTHUR CUTTEN: greatest of the wheat speculators—died insolvent.

RICHARD WHITNEY: eventually president of the New York Stock Exchange—went to Sing Sing prison for embezzlement.

ALBERT FALL: member of a U.S. President's cabinet—went to prison for accepting bribes.

JESS LIVERMORE: greatest "bear" on Wall Street—committed suicide.

LEON FRASER: eventually president of the Bank of International Settlements—committed suicide.

IVAR KREUGER: head of the world's greatest monopoly—committed suicide.

Even Greek millionaire ARISTOTLE ONASSIS, who retained his wealth and died at a ripe old age, recognized that money isn't the same as success. He said, "After you reach a certain point, money becomes unimportant. What matters is success."

FROM *The Success Journey*

Self-trust is the
first secret of success.

—AUTHOR UNKNOWN

BASEBALL DIARY

Years ago a young baseball player's long-ball hitting got the attention of a pro scout, and the boy was offered a contract. When he went off to spring training, he performed well. And each week he wired his mother back at home in Mississippi to inform her of his progress.

WEEK ONE: "Dear Mom, leading all batters. These pitchers aren't so tough."

WEEK TWO: "Dear Mom, looks like I will be starting in infield. Now hitting .500."

WEEK THREE: "Dear Mom, today they started throwing curves. Will be home Friday."

THE SILENT LESSON: TEACHABILITY

I f you see the image of a little man sporting a tiny moustache, carrying a cane, and wearing baggy pants, big clumsy shoes, and a derby hat, you know immediately that it's Charlie Chaplin. Just about everyone recognizes him. In fact, in the 1910s and 1920s, he was the most famous and recognizable person on the planet. If we looked at today's celebrities, the only person even in the same category as him in popularity would be Michael Jordan. And to measure who is the bigger star, we will have to wait another seventy-five years to find out how well everyone remembers Michael.

When Chaplin was born, nobody would have predicted great success for him. Born into poverty as the son of English music hall performers, he found himself on the street as a small child when his mother was institutionalized. After years in workhouses and orphanages, he began working on the stage to support himself. By age seventeen, he was a veteran performer. In 1914, while in his mid-twenties, he worked for Mack Sennett at Keystone Studios in Hollywood making $150 a week. During that first year in the movie business, he made thirty-five films working as an actor, writer, and director. Everyone recognized his talent immediately, and his popularity grew. A year later, he earned $1,250 a week. Then in 1918, he did something unheard of. He signed the entertainment industry's first $1 million contract. He was rich; he was famous; and he was the most powerful filmmaker in the world—at the ripe old age of twenty-nine.

Chaplin was successful because he had great talent and incredible drive. But those traits were fueled by teachability. He continually strived to grow, learn, and perfect his craft. Even when he was the most popular and highest-paid performer in the world, he wasn't content with the status quo.

Chaplin explained his desire to improve to an interviewer:

> When I am watching one of my pictures presented to an audience, I always pay close attention to what they don't laugh at. If, for example, several audiences do not laugh at a stunt I mean to be funny, I at once begin to tear that trick to pieces and try to discover what was wrong in the idea or in the execution of it. If I hear a slight ripple at something I had not expected to be funny, I ask myself why that particular thing got a laugh.

That desire to grow made him successful economically, and it brought a high level of excellence to everything he did. In those early days, Chaplin's work was hailed as marvelous entertainment. As time went by, he was recognized as a comic genius. Today many of his movies are considered masterpieces, and he is appreciated as one of the greatest filmmakers of all time. Screenwriter and film critic James Agee wrote, "The finest pantomime, the deepest emotion, the richest and most poignant poetry were in Chaplin's work."

If Chaplin had replaced his teachability with arrogant self-satisfaction when he became successful, his name would be right up there along with Ford Sterling or Ben Turpin, stars of silent films who are all but forgotten today. But Chaplin kept growing and learning as an actor, director, and eventually film executive. When he learned from experience that filmmakers were at the mercy of studios and distributors, he started his own organization, United Artists, along with Douglas Fairbanks, Mary Pickford, and D. W. Griffith. The film company is still in business today.

FROM *The 21 Indispensable Qualities of a Leader*

Destiny is not a matter of chance,
it is a matter of choice.
It is not a thing to be waited for, it
is a thing to be achieved.

—WILLIAM JENNINGS BRYAN

SPENDING TIME

You don't really pay for things with money.
You pay for them with time.
"In five years, I'll have put enough away
to buy that vacation house we want.
Then I'll slow down."
That means the house will cost you five years—
one-twelfth of your adult life.
Translate the dollar value of the house,
car, or anything else into time,
and then see if it's still worth it. . . .
The phrase *spending your time* is not a metaphor.
It's how life works.

—CHARLES SPEZZANO

Until you value yourself,
you won't value your time.
Until you value your time,
you will not do anything with it.

—M. Scott Peck

It takes a long time to bring excellence to maturity.

—Publilius Syrus

THE TRUE MEASURE OF SUCCESS

To be able to carry money without spending it;
To be able to bear an injustice without retaliating;
To be able to do one's duty when critical eyes watch;
To be able to keep at a job until it is finished;
To be able to do the work and let others receive
 the recognition;
To be able to accept criticism without letting it whip you;
To like those who push you down;
To love when hate is all about you;
To follow God when others put detour signs in your path;
To have a peace of heart and mind because you have given
 God your best.
This is the true measure of success.

—AUTHOR UNKNOWN

Seven Myths of Leadership

The earlier you are in your career, the less likely you are to be in a top-level leadership role. But don't let that stop you. You can start leading right now from the bottom or middle of an organization if you can stretch yourself to overcome these seven myths about leadership.

1. The Position Myth: "I can't lead if I'm not at the top."
2. The Destination Myth: "When I get to the top, then I'll learn to lead."
3. The Influence Myth: "If I were on top, then people would follow me."
4. The Inexperience Myth: "When I get to the top, I'll be in control."
5. The Freedom Myth: "When I get to the top, I'll no longer be limited."
6. The Potential Myth: "I can't reach my potential if I'm not the top leader."
7. The All-Or-Nothing Myth: "If I can't get to the top, then I won't try to lead."

—From *The 360-Degree Leader*

No matter what the circumstances,
our greatest limitation isn't the leader above us—
it's the spirit within us.

—John C. Maxwell

GIVE GOD THE FIRST

Give God the first part of every day.
Give God the first day of every week.
Give God the first portion of your income.
Give God the first consideration in every decision.
Give God the first place in your life.

—JOHN C. MAXWELL

Perhaps it would be a good idea,
fantastic as it sounds,
to muffle every telephone,
stop every motor, and halt all activity
for an hour some day
to give people a chance
to ponder for a few minutes
on what it is all about,
why they are living,
and what they really want.

—JAMES TRUSLOW ADAMS

KEYS TO SUCCESS

THE HOT POKER PRINCIPLE

If you place a poker near the heat of a fire, it becomes hot.
To succeed, follow the hot poker principle.

- *Be around great men and women, and learn from their experiences.*
- *Visit great places.*
- *Attend great events.*
- *Read great books.*

Inside Out

Most people approach success from the outside in. But to achieve real success, you have to do it from the inside out. Focus on your character, and your whole life improves. Changes in character bring substance and power, while external improvements are merely cosmetic and quickly fade away.

Faced with crisis,
the man of character
falls back on himself.
—Charles de Gaulle

Having potential
works exactly opposite to the way
a savings account does.
In a savings account, as time goes by,
your money compounds interest.
The longer you leave it untouched,
the more it increases.

When it comes to potential,
the longer you leave it untouched,
the more it decreases.
Unused potential wastes away.
If you want your potential to increase,
you have to tap into it.

—John C. Maxwell

MAKE ROOM TO GROW

O ne of the most popular aquarium fish is the shark. The reason is that sharks adapt to their environment. If you catch a small shark and confine it, it will stay a size proportionate to the aquarium in which it lives. Sharks can be six inches long yet fully mature. But if you turn them loose in the ocean, they grow to their normal size.

The same is true of potential leaders. Some are put into an organization where the confining environment ensures that they stay small and underdeveloped. That's why it's crucial that you create an environment of growth around you.

That kind of place should look like this:

1. *Others are ahead of you*
2. *You are still challenged*
3. *Your focus is forward*
4. *The atmosphere is affirming*
5. *You are out of your comfort zone*
6. *Others are growing*
7. *There is a willingness to change*
8. *Growth is modeled and expected*

The more positive the environment, the more rapid your growth is able to be. A life of continual growth is never easy, but a good environment makes the swim up stream a little less difficult.

—From *DEVELOPING THE LEADERS AROUND YOU* AND *YOUR ROAD MAP FOR SUCCESS*

An unused life is an early death.

—AUTHOR UNKNOWN

IF YOU WANT HAPPINESS

If you want happiness for an hour—
   take a nap.
If you want happiness for a day—
   go fishing.
If you want happiness for a month—
   get married.
If you want happiness for a year—
   inherit a fortune.
If you want happiness for a lifetime—
   help others.

—CHINESE PROVERB

THE RACE AT SUNRISE

Every morning in Africa, a gazelle wakes up. It knows that it must run faster than the fastest lion, or it will be killed.

Every morning a lion wakes up. It knows that it must outrun the slowest gazelle, or it will starve to death.

It doesn't matter whether you are a lion or a gazelle; when the sun comes up, you had better be running.

—AFRICAN PARABLE

THE TWENTY-FOUR HOUR RULE

Don Shula, former coach of the Miami Dolphins, is the only coach to have led his NFL team to both a perfect season and a Super Bowl victory. His secret? When he coached, he held to a twenty-four hour rule. After a football game, he allowed himself, his coaches, and his players only twenty-four hours to celebrate a victory or sulk over a defeat. During that time, they were encouraged to make the most of the experience. But once the twenty-four hours were over, they had to put it behind them. You don't have to be a football player to benefit from that advice.

There are two types of people
who never achieve much in their lifetime.
The person who won't do what he is told,
and the person who does no more than he is told.

—ANDREW CARNEGIE

The Three "Cs" of Growth

These three words will determine your growth.
Choice—it allows you to *start* growing.
Change—it allows you to *keep* growing.
Climate—it allows you to *enjoy* growing.

I long to accomplish a great and noble task;
but it is my chief duty and job
to accomplish humble tasks
as though they were great and noble.
The world is moved along,
not only by the mighty shoves of its heroes,
but also by the aggregate of the tiny pushes
of each honest worker.

—HELEN KELLER

KEYS TO SUCCESS

The reward for work well done
is the opportunity to do more.

—JONAS SALK

There are no traffic jams on the second mile.

—ZIG ZIGLAR

Acknowledgements

Grateful acknowledgement is made to Thomas
Nelson, Inc. for permission to reprint from the
following books.

Maxwell, John C. 2002. *The 17 Essential Qualities of a
Team Player: Becoming the Kind of Person Every
Team Wants*

Maxwell, John C. 1999. *The 21 Indispensable Qualities
of a Leader: Becoming the Person Others Will Want
to Follow*

Maxwell, John C. 2000. *The 21 Most Powerful Minutes
in a Leader's Day: Revitalize Your Spirit and Empower
Your Leadership*

Maxwell, John C. 2006. *The 360 Degree Leader:
Developing Your Influence from Anywhere in the
Organization*

Maxwell, John C. 2000. *Failing Forward: Turning
Mistakes into Stepping Stones for Success*

Maxwell, John C. 1997. *The Success Journey: The Process
of Living Your Dreams*

Maxwell, John C. 2002. *Your Road Map To Success:
You Can Get There from Here*

ABOUT THE AUTHOR

JOHN C. MAXWELL is an internationally recognized leadership expert, speaker, and author who has sold more than 16 million books. His organizations have trained more than 2 million leaders worldwide. Dr. Maxwell is the founder of EQUIP and INJOY Stewardship Services. Every year he speaks to Fortune 500 companies, international government leaders, and audiences as diverse as the United States Military Academy at West Point, the National Football League, and ambassadors at the United Nations. A *New York Times, Wall Street Journal,* and *Business Week* best-selling author, Maxwell was named the World's Top Leadership Guru by Leadershipgurus.net. He was one of only twenty-five authors and artists named to Amazon.com's 10th Anniversary Hall of Fame. Three of his books, *The 21 Irrefutable Laws of Leadership, Developing the Leader Within You,* and *The 21 Indispensable Qualities of a Leader,* have each sold more than a million copies.